QUESTIONS EXPLORED

WHAT IS ANXIETY?

by Philip Wolny

BrightPoint Press

San Diego, CA

© 2023 BrightPoint Press
an imprint of ReferencePoint Press, Inc.
Printed in the United States

For more information, contact:
BrightPoint Press
PO Box 27779
San Diego, CA 92198
www.BrightPointPress.com

ALL RIGHTS RESERVED.

No part of this work covered by the copyright hereon may be reproduced or used in any form or by any means—graphic, electronic, or mechanical, including photocopying, recording, taping, web distribution, or information storage retrieval systems—without the written permission of the publisher.

Content Consultant: Jessica Bodie, PhD, Perelman School of Medicine, University of Pennsylvania

---

LIBRARY OF CONGRESS CATALOGING-IN-PUBLICATION DATA

Names: Wolny, Philip, author.
Title: What is anxiety? / by Philip Wolny.
Description: San Diego, CA: BrightPoint Press, [2023] | Series: Questions
  explored | Includes bibliographical references and index. | Audience:
  Grades 7-9
Identifiers: LCCN 2022029132 (print) | LCCN 2022029133 (eBook) | ISBN
  9781678205065 (hardcover) | ISBN 9781678205072 (pdf)
Subjects: LCSH: Anxiety--Juvenile literature. |
  Anxiety--Treatment--Juvenile literature.
Classification: LCC BF575.A6 W66 2023 (print) | LCC BF575.A6 (eBook) |
  DDC 152.4/6--dc23/eng/20220630
LC record available at https://lccn.loc.gov/2022029132
LC eBook record available at https://lccn.loc.gov/2022029133

CONTENTS

AT A GLANCE   4

INTRODUCTION   6
    WHEN FEAR TAKES OVER

CHAPTER ONE   12
    WHAT IS ANXIETY?

CHAPTER TWO   30
    WHERE DOES ANXIETY COME FROM?

CHAPTER THREE   44
    HOW CAN PEOPLE DEAL WITH ANXIETY?

CHAPTER FOUR   60
    WHAT ARE DIFFERENT WAYS TO FIGHT ANXIETY?

Glossary	74
Source Notes	75
For Further Research	76
Index	78
Image Credits	79
About the Author	80

AT A GLANCE

- Anxiety is the most common mental health issue among Americans. It has become a major concern for young children, teenagers, and college-age youth.

- Anxiety is a normal human emotion. Everyone gets anxious, and dealing with anxiety is a regular part of growing up.

- Anxiety becomes concerning when it takes up a great deal of someone's time and mental energy. It is especially worrying when it interferes with someone's daily life and prevents them from functioning properly.

- Anxiety arises from signals in the body that are meant to respond to danger. When anxiety becomes severe, it can cause panic attacks, depression, and other negative effects.

- Anxiety can have both physical and mental effects.

- The first major step to combat anxiety and anxiety disorders is a proper diagnosis for the condition. Health professionals such as psychiatrists, psychologists, and therapists can diagnose anxiety.

- There are several types of treatment for anxiety. Therapy is among the most important, and it is often the first line of treatment.

- More serious or longer-lasting forms of anxiety can be treated with prescription medications. Doctors such as psychiatrists prescribe such medications. Medications can work alongside therapy.

INTRODUCTION

WHEN FEAR TAKES OVER

Alex wakes up on a school day. She goes downstairs for breakfast. Right away, she notices that her older brother Dan is not in the kitchen like usual. She hears him arguing with their parents. He does not want to go to school. He thinks the teachers and other kids will look at him funny. He worries that the bus will crash.

Many people find that their anxiety makes them more irritable. They might get upset easily or argue with others.

Lately, when Dan gets home, he disappears into his room. On weekends, he sleeps late. He goes to bed very early.

People with anxiety may feel easily tired or sleep to avoid anxious thoughts.

His friends used to call and visit. But now they rarely do.

Alex is worried. Dan seemed perfectly fine just weeks ago. She thinks her parents have not noticed how he has changed. They both work such long hours.

When Dan argues with them, they usually back off. Sometimes they tell him he is just imagining things. One day, their mom had a hard day at the office. She told Dan to just get over his worries. Dan got up quietly and went back to his room.

That night, Alex streams a television show about anxiety. Many of the people on the show act like her brother. Alex goes to her school library and asks for some books on anxiety. She also does some online searches at home.

Alex starts to think that her brother Dan has a problem. It seems like his anxiety is something he cannot handle on his own. "Just getting over it" will definitely not be enough.

She decides to gather a few books and some printouts of online articles. She plans to leave them in a box for her parents. She will talk to her brother too. Alex feels better now that she has a plan. She wants to understand what Dan is going through. She thinks she can help her family find a better way to handle anxiety.

Being a good listener is just one way to support someone with anxiety.

CHAPTER ONE

WHAT IS ANXIETY?

Anxiety is an emotion that everyone feels. It can be normal and healthy. Worrying about things is only natural.

Students might wake up worried about taking a test. They might spend the day concerned about doing well. Their anxiety only ends when they have turned in their tests.

Many people get anxious about taking a big test.

Young people may worry about sports competitions or acting in a school play. Starting a new school year might be stressful. So is moving to a new neighborhood, city, or country.

Adults also experience anxiety. They may get stressed about traffic on the way

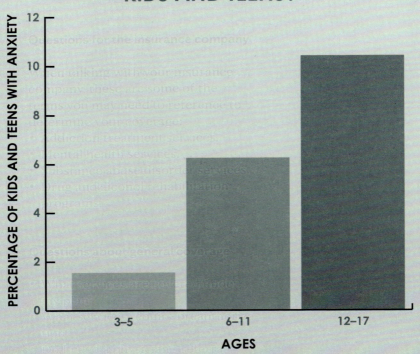

Among kids and teens, young people from ages twelve to seventeen have the highest rates of anxiety and anxiety disorders.

to work. A doctor visit about a new health issue can make them anxious. Losing a job can worry them too.

WHEN TO WORRY (ABOUT WORRYING)

It is natural to worry about stressful things. This kind of anxiety is expected and normal. Everyone feels it sometimes. Dealing with it is an important part of growing up.

Normal anxiety is related to a specific problem or situation. It lasts only as long as the problem itself lasts. The amount of anxiety makes sense. It matches how serious the problem is.

But anxiety can take over one's thoughts. Test-takers may worry about forgetting everything they studied. They panic instead of preparing for the test. Worrying about

Many kids and teens struggle with anxiety.

doing badly can actually make them do worse.

An anxious person is often worried, nervous, or afraid about everyday life. They might get anxious with little or no warning. Their anxiety might not have a cause or reason at all.

If someone feels anxiety a lot of the time, it might mean that they have an anxiety disorder. Around 40 million adults in the United States are believed to have one. That is about 18.1 percent of the population. Studies show that anxiety affects about 25.1 percent of US children ages thirteen to eighteen.

Many anxiety sufferers constantly think of problems. They stress about unlikely or impossible events. Even when a problem has passed, they often cannot shake their anxiety. They may replay it in their minds. It can be hard to control.

Dodging a dodgeball in gym class is an example of the fight-or-flight response.

FIGHT, FLIGHT, OR FREEZE

Thousands of years ago, humans dealt with many physical dangers. For example, someone might have run into a hungry wolf or wild cat. Humans evolved to deal with these dangers.

Sudden danger can sometimes **trigger** the fight-or-flight response. People make a quick decision. They may try to fight or scare off a threat. This is the fight response. Or they can choose to run away. This is the flight response. People in a dangerous situation might also freeze up. They are stuck in one place or position.

In stressful situations, the body releases special chemicals called hormones. Hormones focus the body and mind to deal with threats. This might have given an ancient hunter improved hearing, vision, or speed.

People in the modern world deal with the fight-or-flight response too. Students playing dodgeball react quickly. They jump out of the way of the ball. Seeing an unfriendly dog or another possible danger in the street can also trigger it.

Sometimes the fight-or-flight response happens when something is not really dangerous. This is called a "false alarm." For example, a person with an anxiety disorder might have a strong reaction to hearing a balloon pop. This may lead him to avoid situations that are actually safe, such as a party with balloons.

A "false alarm" might cause someone to avoid certain situations.

TYPES OF ANXIETY

Different types of anxiety can affect people differently. Some people experience anxiety for long periods of time. Others find that it comes and goes. Different life events can trigger anxiety.

Some people are anxious about many aspects of daily life. This condition is known as generalized anxiety disorder (GAD). People with GAD worry about things such as their health, making mistakes, and being on time. Worrying about these things is understandable. But for people with GAD, these worries feel uncontrollable. They can make people feel restless, tired, or grumpy. They can get in the way of living life.

Social anxiety disorder, or social phobia, is another category of anxiety.

Socially anxious people are nervous about things done in public. They often worry about what people will think of them.

ANXIETY AT PARTIES

It can be exciting to get invited to a party. But it can be different for kids with anxiety. April Marie Gott Walker is a parenting blogger. She writes that for her son, a party means, "I have to go to a new environment and be surrounded by new people, and stress about the unknowns of an event that I have no control over for the next two weeks." Kids with anxiety might spend the party avoiding other kids. They may feel miserable and want their parent nearby. Anxiety can make it hard to have fun.

Quoted in April Marie Gott Walker, "Birthday Parties Are Hard for Kids with Anxiety, but It Doesn't Have to Be a Disaster," Scary Mommy, *January 10, 2017. www.scarymommy.com.*

They may fear eating or drinking around others. They might have a deep fear of public speaking. It is hard for them to meet new people.

Another type of anxiety is panic disorder. Almost everyone has had a moment of extreme panic. These moments can be scary, but they eventually pass. These episodes are called panic attacks. They might only happen once or twice. Someone who keeps having them and worries about the next one may have a panic disorder. The panic might come out of nowhere. It can make the person feel like he cannot breathe. It might give him chest pain, dizziness, and a racing heart.

Another related condition is obsessive-compulsive disorder (OCD). OCD sufferers have strong fears. They perform certain behaviors over and over again to try to ease

---

PHOBIAS

When people are very afraid of something, they may have a specific phobia. Some common phobias include heights, needles, and small spaces. For people with a phobia, situations involving their fears cause high levels of anxiety. They try to avoid these situations. Their fears are often too intense to "get over" on their own. But a therapist can help people learn to manage their phobias.

Some OCD sufferers have an extreme fear of germs and might clean things repeatedly.

their anxiety. They might worry that they are unclean and wash their hands many times a day. Others might worry that they have lost something. They might check their pockets every thirty seconds for their phones or keys.

OCD patients have obsessive, unpleasant thoughts. These can interfere with regular life. British university student Lizzie Green discussed her OCD with Huffington Post. She dealt with it for ten years before getting diagnosed. Green said,

> Without even realising what I was doing, my life compiled of obsessive rituals, unnecessarily repeating actions and steps. . . . Everything would take me double the amount of time needed, and I was completely consumed by thoughts. My thoughts stemmed from 'if I didn't do this certain action that

my mind was telling me to, something "bad" would happen."[1]

Often, OCD sufferers know their obsessions do not follow logic. But they still struggle to stop them.

Post-traumatic stress disorder (PTSD) is another common condition related to anxiety. It can happen after someone experiences a stressful event. A car crash, medical emergency, or abuse can lead to PTSD. Military veterans and first responders dealing with emergencies can also suffer from it. Sufferers may experience flashbacks or nightmares. They may be

PTSD sufferers may be triggered by sights, sounds, smells, or situations that remind them of the trauma they experienced.

jumpy or irritable. They may get upset when

reminded of the **trauma**.

CHAPTER TWO

WHERE DOES ANXIETY COME FROM?

Anxiety has many different causes. Sometimes it can be a normal response to life's situations and problems. But in some cases, it can get so bad that it stops someone from living a confident, healthy life.

Many people who deal with bullying develop anxiety disorders.

WORRYING AT SCHOOL AND AT HOME

School might be one cause of anxiety. Children and teens sometimes stress about getting good grades. Student athletes might worry about making a team. Every game or match might make them anxious.

Other school problems also cause anxiety. A student may have trouble making friends or fitting in. Dealing with bullying might make someone anxious. Such fears can make someone avoid school. Eighteen-year-old Tyler Chabot told a newspaper about how he left a gifted program in fifth grade. The pressure made

Family troubles or stress at home may cause anxiety.

him anxious. In his new class, he was

bullied for being the kid from the gifted

program. "I needed help but I didn't know

how to ask for it," Chabot said. By eighth grade, he stopped going to school. "I would pretend to go and then I'd take the bus back home."[2]

Issues at home or in the family can also be stressful. These can be regular, everyday problems. People may not get along with their parents. They might fight with their siblings.

More serious issues lead to more serious anxiety. A young person might deal with very bad situations or experiences. These are called trauma. Getting into a car accident is traumatic. So is having a parent or relative get very sick or even die. Substance abuse in a family can also cause anxiety. The memory of trauma stays with people for a long time. The pain and emotions that come with that memory are part of trauma too.

ANXIETY FROM THE NEWS

Paying too much attention to negative news can be harmful. It can make someone think the world is a scary, dangerous place. This can cause anxiety. Many people think that more information will make them feel in control. But the opposite is often true. Experts say people should limit how much bad news they consume. They should ask themselves if a news story is providing new information. If not, it is probably just adding to their anxiety.

Restlessness and trembling are both physical symptoms of anxiety.

ANXIETY AND THE BODY

People feel anxiety in their bodies. They might feel their breathing and heartbeats speed up. Their hands get sweatier than normal. Muscles tighten and tense up. An anxious person's leg might shake.

Trembling is another sign of anxiety. So is restlessness. Anxious people can find it hard to focus. They might be able to think only about their anxiety.

Some anxiety sufferers experience dizziness. Their legs might get weak. They may find it hard to swallow. Stomach problems such as nausea are common too. Anxiety can cause loss of appetite.

Worrying can also tire people out. Staying in bed may seem easier than facing

Some people with anxiety suffer from insomnia.

the world. People with anxiety might feel weak or tired all the time.

For others, the opposite is true. Their anxiety actually causes **insomnia**. They are unable to fall asleep and might spend hours awake at night. Lack of sleep can cause even more anxiety.

ANXIETY AND DAILY LIFE

Feeling anxiety all the time can be tough for anyone. It can be especially hard for a kid or teenager. Growing up is already a time

---

AGORAPHOBIA AND SEPARATION ANXIETY

One kind of anxiety disorder is called **agoraphobia**. People with agoraphobia are scared of leaving their homes or being in wide open spaces. Agoraphobia can happen alongside separation anxiety. This is when someone is afraid of being away from parents or family. Child psychologist Dr. Jamie Howard says, "People with agoraphobia worry that something bad will happen and then they'll be out in the world, unsafe, unable to escape, and there will be no one who can help them."

Quoted in Rachel Ehmke, "Agoraphobia in Children," Child Mind Institute, n.d. www.childmind.org.

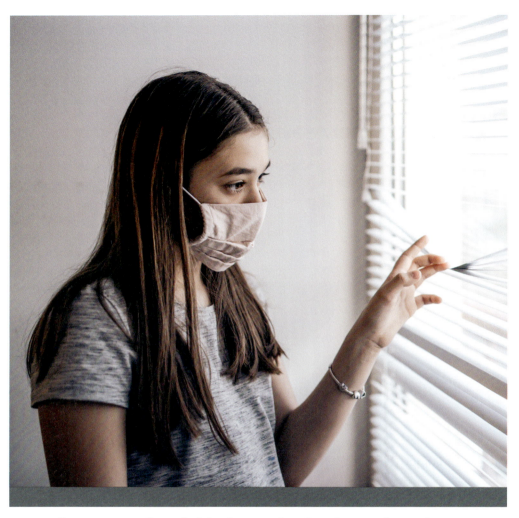

Some people might choose to stay home in order to avoid situations that make them anxious.

of great change. Anxious youth can react differently than their peers to things that stress them out.

Anxious people might find social situations tough to handle. They might be shy and quieter than others around them. In other cases, they might become louder and more emotional.

People with anxiety might find it hard to do their schoolwork. Having many worries and fears can make it hard to approach things they used to enjoy. They may avoid friends, favorite activities, or even leaving the house.

ROOTS, CAUSES, AND SIDE EFFECTS

Researchers think that some kinds of anxiety are **hereditary**. That is, someone

Many people with anxiety also suffer from depression.

whose parent has serious anxiety may be more likely to develop it themselves. The person could inherit characteristics from a parent that could lead to anxiety. Being raised by an anxious parent might also be a factor. A child with a parent who behaves anxiously might be more likely to act the same way.

Anxiety is linked to other mental health issues too. People who suffer from depression, alcohol or drug abuse, or other conditions might have anxiety. Anxiety can be a root cause of such conditions. Sometimes it can make them worse. Experts believe as many as 60 percent of anxiety sufferers may also have symptoms of depression.

CHAPTER THREE

HOW CAN PEOPLE DEAL WITH ANXIETY?

Regular anxiety comes and goes. Anxiety disorders often stick around. Someone with symptoms may have difficulty figuring out the difference. A young person might not even realize they have anxiety. Sometimes, symptoms that look like anxiety might be something else.

Teens who feel anxious should talk to a trusted adult for help.

Identifying the problem is the best first step. It is also up to parents to pay attention. Psychiatrist Dr. Valerie Arnold points out, "Because anxious children may also be quiet and eager to please, parents should be alert to the signs of severe anxiety."[3] This way, they can help treat their children.

An anxious young person can go to someone they feel safe around. They might tell a parent, grandparent, or older sibling. Others might be more comfortable with a teacher or school counselor.

ANXIETY IN TIMES OF CRISIS

Anxiety can become a big issue during a national crisis or emergency. An example is the COVID-19 pandemic that began in 2020. During this time, anxiety in young people and teens increased. People feared the virus. Schools were shut down. Many felt the trauma of losing family members and friends. In such times, it is important for kids to speak out about what they are experiencing. Parents and other adults can only help if they realize the scope of the problem.

A PROFESSIONAL DIAGNOSIS

Diagnosing anxiety is best left to professionals. This means seeing a psychiatrist, psychologist, therapist, or social worker. They ask questions about the patient's experiences. This helps them find out what triggers the patient's anxiety and how it gets in the way. Doctors may also ask about the patient's activities, performance at school, or diet.

A doctor will ask about a patient's medical history too. They may explore the medical history of the patient's parents and other family members. This is to rule out or identify any other physical diseases or conditions. Doctors also need to ask about any medications a patient is taking. Certain medications can increase anxiety.

The process works best when patients are open and honest about their experiences and feelings. One easy way is through diagnostic questionnaires. These are tests where the patient answers specific questions. Patients are asked to rate their anxiety. Questions ask about shaking, sweating, nervousness, and more. These tests help doctors make an accurate **diagnosis**.

Doctors can help patients figure out the best way to treat their anxiety.

A doctor completes a diagnosis mostly by talking with the patient and collecting information. Patients talk about their fears, moods, and physical and mental anxiety symptoms.

TREATING ANXIETY

There are different ways to treat anxiety disorders. Therapy is one way. Going to therapy means talking through one's problems with a therapist. Therapists help patients understand their anxiety and learn to manage it.

Another option is taking medication. Most medications for anxiety are prescribed by psychiatrists. The treatment depends on how serious the disorder is. It also depends on the person. Everyone's needs are different. Some people need only therapy. Others get by with medication. A doctor

Therapy can help someone learn to effectively manage their anxiety.

might even prescribe lifestyle changes such as exercise or self-care. Usually, combining medication and therapy is the most effective option for treating anxiety. Child psychologist Dr. Eli Lebowitz says, "In cases of severe anxiety the most sensible thing may often be to start combined treatment right away."[4]

HOW THERAPY CAN HELP

There are different kinds of therapy. A therapist will fit the right kind to the patient. This can depend on whether the patient is a child, teen, or adult.

One of the most common kinds of anxiety treatment is called cognitive behavioral therapy (CBT). CBT helps someone change how they see their anxiety and how they respond to it. Therapists guide patients like a coach. They help them practice facing their fears. This teaches the patient's brain to see the difference between "false alarms" and real danger.

Exposure therapy helps patients learn to face their fears.

It also helps patients change how they react to anxiety in the future.

Exposure therapy is the leading form of CBT for anxiety. Exposures are practice exercises in which people face their fears. They are designed to be safe and help people overcome their fears. For example,

A patient with social anxiety might practice public speaking during exposure therapy.

someone with social anxiety might be afraid of speaking in front of crowds. The person's therapist might have her practice speaking in public. A therapist treating panic attacks might ask a patient to breathe through a straw rapidly. This causes shortness of breath and dizziness. These feelings are similar to what the patient feels during a "false alarm" panic attack. This shows him that these feelings are safe and normal. Over time, the patient reacts less strongly to these feelings. He has fewer panic attacks.

    Therapists often organize exposures from the least stressful to most stressful exercises. That way, the patient's confidence builds. Someone with a dog phobia can practice looking at a dog through a window. Then she can stand near a dog on a leash. Finally, she can pet a dog. The more patients are safely exposed to something, the less they will fear it.

Some anxiety patients benefit from a combination of therapy and medication.

CBT and other kinds of therapy usually happen on a regular basis. This can mean a one-on-one meeting once a week with a mental health professional. A therapist might plan visits more than once a week if the patient needs them. Most therapists see a patient for forty-five to sixty minutes per visit.

Therapy can be short-term. It could last a few weeks or months. Some patients might benefit from staying in treatment for years. Others might make appointments only when their disorders worsen. It all depends on the patient and his or her doctor's treatment plan.

MEDICATION FOR ANXIETY

Some patients need more than therapy to cope with their anxiety. Psychiatrists can prescribe medication for anxiety and related conditions. They work with patients and their parents or guardians. Together, they figure out how much medication a patient needs. They also decide how long the patient should take the medication. This depends on how seriously anxiety affects the patient. **Antidepressants** are the most common drugs used to treat anxiety. They help control a patient's mood, sleep

> ### TYPES OF ANTIDEPRESSANTS
>
> There are two common types of antidepressants. These are selective serotonin reuptake inhibitors (SSRIs) and serotonin-norepinephrine reuptake inhibitors (SNRIs). Serotonin is a chemical in the brain. It affects happiness and mood. SSRIs and SNRIs both increase the amount of serotonin in the brain. This helps ease symptoms of anxiety and depression.

patterns, and appetite. It can take as long as twelve weeks for antidepressants to begin working fully. But many start to work within two weeks.

Other drugs used to treat anxiety include benzodiazepines. These drugs calm people down and reduce muscle tension. Doctors prescribe them for patients who need very quick results. But these medications have risks. They should not be used long-term. Some anxiety patients may also be prescribed antipsychotic drugs. These drugs balance brain chemicals.

CHAPTER FOUR

WHAT ARE DIFFERENT WAYS TO FIGHT ANXIETY?

Some people deal with anxiety for months and years at a time. Other people might experience it on and off their whole lives. Whatever the case may be, experts agree that there are many different ways to fight anxiety.

Breathing exercises can help someone calm down when they feel anxious.

BREATH AND MUSCLE CONTROL

There are several things people can do on their own to fight anxiety. This is true whether they have gotten professional treatment yet or not. The easiest one is breathing exercises. These can be done right when someone starts to feel anxious. Breathing in and out slowly can calm a person down. So can counting down from ten to one.

Muscle tension is a sign of anxiety. Some people can feel it even before they realize that they are anxious. Doing exercises can

JUST BREATHE

"Square breathing" is one kind of breathing exercise. A person slowly breathes in, taking four seconds. Then they hold their breath for the same amount of time. They breathe out for another four seconds and then pause. Then they start the cycle again. Someone can do this for minutes at a time. Doing so can relax the mind and the body.

reduce stress. People can start by sitting down on the floor or on an exercise mat. Then they tense each muscle. Some people find it helpful to squeeze and relax muscles in order. They begin with the toes. Then they move up to the calves and thighs. They keep going, from the stomach, to the arms and shoulders, and to the neck. They should do it smoothly, without using too much effort. They should pay attention to flexing the muscle and then relaxing it. They can take ten seconds for each muscle group. These exercises can be done when someone is anxious. They can also reduce future anxiety.

WRITE IT OUT AND SAY IT LOUD

Therapists often recommend that patients use their own voices as part of their treatments. This technique allows them to see their anxiety in a new way. By doing this, patients can more easily manage their anxiety.

One idea is to keep a journal or diary. People write about their experiences with anxiety. They add their thoughts and feelings. Writing the journal and reading it over later are both important. This can

Journaling is a good way for someone to track her symptoms.

help people figure out their anxiety triggers. Triggers are things that bring on anxiety.

Journals also help people review and improve their progress. They can keep track of coping techniques, such as breathing and muscle relaxation. They can read the journal to see what worked and what did not work when they last had a panic attack.

Other people might use self-talk therapy. This means they try to have a conversation

ART AS THERAPY

Creativity can help reduce stress and anxiety. Drawing, painting, photography, and music are just some of the artistic activities that can help. Describing anxiety is hard to put into words sometimes. Art can help someone understand and relieve those feelings. Whether or not the art is about anxiety, expressing oneself can be very calming. Many clinics and hospitals that treat mental health use art therapy.

with themselves. People with anxiety may hear a negative voice in their heads. Often, it is the main voice they listen to. Talking back to that voice can help.

Therapist Jeffrey Nevid points out, "Have you ever talked back to the voices in your head? Have you ever stopped for a moment and said to yourself, 'Wait a minute. Why am I thinking that way? Must it be so? Might there be another way of thinking about [something]?'"[5]

This technique helps fight automatic, negative thoughts. For example, a student's first thought might be, "I'm going to fail this exam." The student might respond, "I have been studying for days. How bad could I do?"

AN OUNCE OF PREVENTION

There are many things people can do to lessen anxiety in their lives. One of these is physical activity. Riding a bike, taking a dance or martial arts class, or going for a walk are great options.

Daily exercises at home also help. These include working with weights, doing sit-ups and push-ups, and stretching. Young people can ask trusted adults or their physical education teachers for tips.

Exercising and spending time outside can ease symptoms of anxiety.

They can also watch videos online to find instructions for different activities.

Harvard professor Dr. John Ratey writes, "Lacing up your sneakers and getting out and moving may be the single best nonmedical solution we have for preventing and treating anxiety."[6] Exercise is a great distraction from anxiety. It lessens muscle tension. An increased heart rate helps release brain chemicals that fight anxiety. Exercise also helps the brain areas that control the fight-or-flight response. Physical fitness can even prevent anxiety symptoms from happening in the first place.

MAINTAINING AND THRIVING

There is no simple fix for anxiety. It is important for anxiety patients to stick to a treatment plan. It can take time to see results. Sticking to it helps a person figure out if the plan is right for them.

It is important for anxiety sufferers to stay engaged with their friends and hobbies.

Many people suffering from anxiety have been told "it's all in your mind." In some ways, this is true. Worry comes from the brain. But with practice, people can learn to face situations and thoughts that trigger them. They can find ways to stay active with friends, family, and favorite activities.

Eating a healthy, balanced diet can help ease anxiety symptoms.

This can help a person stop avoiding those situations.

Healthy eating can help too. Skipping meals can affect a person's blood sugar and mood. It is important to drink enough water. Too much caffeine can worsen anxiety. Consuming alcohol, nicotine, or other drugs can also make a person's anxiety worse.

Managing anxiety is a lifelong effort. There are ups and downs. Learning how to cope with it is important. It is also important to diagnose and treat anxiety disorders. The rewards include fewer worries and a happier, healthier life.

GLOSSARY

agoraphobia

extreme fear of leaving the home, or of being in open or crowded places

antidepressants

a class of medications that mainly help a patient fight depression but have also been found to work to fight anxiety

diagnosis

identifying a person's illness or medical condition through tests, questions, and symptoms

hereditary

describing something that is passed on from parents to their children, like hair color or other traits

insomnia

difficulty falling or staying asleep

trauma

a disturbing event that a person experiences or witnesses and which affects their mental health

trigger

to cause a strong emotional reaction; an action or situation that causes anxiety, an emotional response, or another mental health issue

SOURCE NOTES

CHAPTER ONE: WHAT IS ANXIETY?

1. Quoted in Lucy Sherriff, "Why You're Probably Not 'So OCD'. Here's What It's *Really* Like to Have It," *Huffington Post*, May 21, 2015. www.huffingtonpost.co.uk.

CHAPTER TWO: WHERE DOES ANXIETY COME FROM?

2. Quoted in Denise Davy, "Kids, Poverty and Mental Health: Anxiety a Growing Problem," *CBC News*, February 19, 2014. www.cbc.ca.

CHAPTER THREE: HOW CAN PEOPLE DEAL WITH ANXIETY?

3. Quoted in "Anxiety in Adolescents and Teens," *Le Bonheur Children's Hospital,* July 18, 2018. www.lebonheur.org.

4. Quoted in Bill Hathaway, "Severe Anxiety Best Treated with Drugs and Therapy," *YaleNews*, October 2, 2017. https://news.yale.edu.

CHAPTER FOUR: WHAT ARE DIFFERENT WAYS TO FIGHT ANXIETY?

5. Quoted in Jeffrey S. Nevid, "Talking Back to Yourself," *Psychology Today*, December 31, 2015. www.psychologytoday.com.

6. Quoted in John J. Ratey, "Can Exercise Help Treat Anxiety?" *Harvard Health Publishing*, October 24, 2019. www.health.harvard.edu.

FOR FURTHER RESEARCH

BOOKS

Celina McManus, *Understanding Anxiety*. San Diego, CA: BrightPoint Press, 2021.

Rachael Morlock, *What Is Social Anxiety?* New York: PowerKids Press, 2021.

Maddie Spalding, *Understanding Phobias*. San Diego, CA: BrightPoint Press, 2021.

INTERNET SOURCES

"Mental Health Resources for Adolescents and Young Adults," *Society for Adolescent Health and Medicine,* n.d. www.adolescenthealth.org.

Caroline Miller, "How Anxiety Affects Teenagers," *Child Mind Institute*, n.d. www.childmind.org.

Diana Rodriguez, "How to Cope with Anxiety and Depression," *Everyday Health*, September 29, 2020. www.everydayhealth.com.

WEBSITES

Anxiety and Depression Association of America (ADAA)
https://adaa.org

The Anxiety and Depression Association of America is an international nonprofit association with the mission of prevention, treatment, and cure of anxiety, depression, OCD, and PTSD.

Anxiety.org
www.anxiety.org

Anxiety.org is a portal for exploring information about anxiety and finding practitioners specializing in different kinds of anxiety disorder treatments. This website also has quizzes, self-diagnostic tests, and other resources.

National Alliance on Mental Illness (NAMI)
www.nami.org/About-Mental-Illness/Mental-Health-Conditions/Anxiety-Disorders

The National Alliance on Mental Illness is the United States' largest grassroots mental health organization dedicated to combating mental illness. NAMI works to educate the public and advocate for people with mental illness.

INDEX

agoraphobia, 39
antidepressants, 58–59
Arnold, Valerie, 45

breathing exercises, 61–62

Chabot, Tyler, 32–34

depression, 43, 58
diagnoses, 47–49
diagnostic questionnaires, 48

exercises, 62–64, 68–70

false alarms, 20, 52, 55
fight-or-flight response, 18–20, 70

generalized anxiety disorder (GAD), 22
Green, Lizzie, 27–28

hormones, 19
Howard, Jamie, 39

insomnia, 38

Lebowitz, Eli, 51

medications, 50–51, 57–59

Nevid, Jeffrey, 67

obsessive compulsive disorder (OCD), 25–28

panic attacks, 24–25, 54–55
panic disorder, 24–25
phobias, 25
post-traumatic stress disorder (PTSD), 28–29

Ratey, John, 69

social anxiety disorder, 22–24, 54

therapies, 50–51, 52–55, 56–57, 66–67
  cognitive behavioral therapy (CBT), 52–56
  exposure therapy, 53–55
  self-talk therapy, 66–68
therapists, 25, 47, 50–51, 52, 54–55, 56–57
triggers, 65

Walker, April Marie Gott, 23

IMAGE CREDITS

Cover: © New Africa/Shutterstock Images
5: © Mdurson/iStockphoto
7: © Yor Ven/iStockphoto
8: © Raw Pixel/Shutterstock Images
11: © Stefan Amer/iStockphoto
13: © Antonio Diaz/Shutterstock Images
14: © Red Line Editorial
16: © Prostock Studio/iStockphoto
18: © Monkey Business Images/iStockphoto
21: © The Visuals You Need/Shutterstock Images
26: © Srdjan Randjelovic/Shutterstock Images
29: © Artist GND Photography/iStockphoto
31: © Daisy Daisy/Shutterstock Images
33: © EJ White/iStockphoto
36: © Katarzyna Bialasiewicz/iStockphoto
38: © The Visuals You Need/Shutterstock Images
40: © Valentin Russanov/iStockphoto
42: © Fizkes/Shutterstock Images
45: © Monkey Business Images/Shutterstock Images
49: © VH Studio/Shutterstock Images
51: © Light Field Studios/Shutterstock Images
53: © Seventy-Four/Shutterstock Images
54: © Urbazon/iStockphoto
56: © Stefan Amer/iStockphoto
61: © Sergey Dementyev/iStockphoto
65: © Odua Images/Shutterstock Images
69: © Sol Stock/iStockphoto
71: © Monkey Business Images/Shutterstock Images
72: © Art Marie/iStockphoto

ABOUT THE AUTHOR

Philip Wolny is an editor, author, and copy editor. Some of his works for young readers include books on space travel, the solar system, the Black Lives Matter movement, the Second Amendment, and drug addiction. He has also written about history, culture, and career preparation.